Zlatan after scoring an absolutely magnificent goal against England on November 22, 2012. He scored four goals in the match!

ZLATAN

Abbeville Press Publishers

New York · London

A portion of the book's proceeds are donated to the **Hugo Bustamante AYSO Playership Fund,** a national scholarship program to help ensure that no child misses the chance to play AYSO Soccer. Donations to the fund cover the cost of registration and a uniform for a child in need.

Text by Illugi Jökulsson

For the original edition
Design and layout: Ólafur Gunnar Guðlaugsson

For the English-language edition
Editor: Joan Strasbaugh
Production manager: Louise Kurtz
Designer: Ada Rodriguez
Copy editor: Ken Samuelson

PHOTOGRAPHY CREDITS

Getty Images
20, 21 Sweden – Portugal, EUFA 2004: Sandra Behne. 22, 23 In Match with Ajax, September 2, 2002: Ben Radford. 38, 89 With AC Milan against Siena in Italy December 2011: Marco Luzzani. 40, 41 Tattoo, taken in April 2012: Marco Luzzani. 42, 43 The Family: Marco Luzzani. 48, 49 With a New Team: Marc Piasecki. 52, 53 Paris Saint-Germain: Xavier Laine.

Shutterstock
2, 3, 8, 9, 12, 13, 14, 15, 16, 17, 24, 25, 26, 27, 28, 29, 32, 33, 34, 35, 36, 37, 44, 45, 46, 47, 50, 51, 54, 55, 56, 57, 58, 59, 60, 62, 62, 63.

Ívar Gissurarson
10, 11, except Young Zlatan: Image from Sydsvenskan. 18, 19 Images from Zlatan's Home Field in Malmö. 30, 31 His House in Malmö. 56 Badge of Honor

Sydsvenskan
12 Young Zlatan.

Bildbyran Malmö
19 Zlatan in a Match with Malmö.

All statistics current through the 2012–2013 season unless otherwise noted.

First published in the United States of America in 2014 by Abbeville Press, 137 Varick Street, New York, NY 10013

First published in Iceland in 2012 by Sögur útgáfa, Fákafen 9, 108 Reykjavík, Iceland

First edition
10 9 8 7 6 5 4 3 2 1

Library of Congress Cataloging-in-Publication Data

Illugi Jvkulsson.
  [Zlatan Ibrahimovic. English]
  Zlatan / by Illugi Jvkulsson. —First edition.
    pages cm. — (World soccer legends)
  Translated from Icelandic.
  Summary: "A complete profile of Swedish football star Zlatan Ibrahimovic. Includes information about his childhood, a record of his famous goals, his successes and disappointments with Barcelona, his family and a discussion of his future as a living legend"—Provided by publisher.
  ISBN 978-0-7892-1169-9 (hardback) —ISBN 0-7892-1169-6 (hardcover) 1. Ibrahimovic, Zlatan, 1981—Juvenile literature. 2. Soccer players—Sweden—Biography—Juvenile literature. I. Illugi Jvkulsson. Zlatan Ibrahimovic. Translation of: II. Title.
   GV942.7.I27I45 2014
   796.334092—dc23
   [B]
                              2013045841

For bulk and premium sales and for text adoption procedures, write to Customer Service Manager, Abbeville Press, 137 Varick Street, New York, NY 10013, or call 1-800-ARTBOOK.

Visit Abbeville Press online at **www.abbeville.com.**

CONTENTS

MALMÖ
ZLATAN'S CITY

If Zlatan Ibrahimovic had been born before 1658, he would have become a Danish citizen and therefore would have played with the Danish national team. This is because the southernmost part of Sweden, called Scania, used to belong to the Danes. However, organized soccer matches were not being played anywhere in the world at that time, so this idea would never have been possible anyway!

The city was originally used as a harbor by the archbishop in Lund. During those times, the name of the city was *Malmhaug*, which could be translated roughly as "a pile of gravel," or "Ore (metal) Hill." The name gradually changed into *Malmö*, which means "Ore Island," even though the city isn't actually built on an island. Malmö's residents were merely a few thousand in the beginning, up until the 18th century, when a bustling harbor had emerged and as a result the population grew steadily. In the 19th century, the Kockums shipyard was built and it became the third largest shipyard in Sweden, after Stockholm and Gothenburg.

This is how Malmö looked in the year 1580.

The Öresund Bridge was opened in the year 2000 and connects Copenhagen and Malmö.

The skyscraper Turning Torso is one of the central landmarks of Malmö. It was completed in 2005

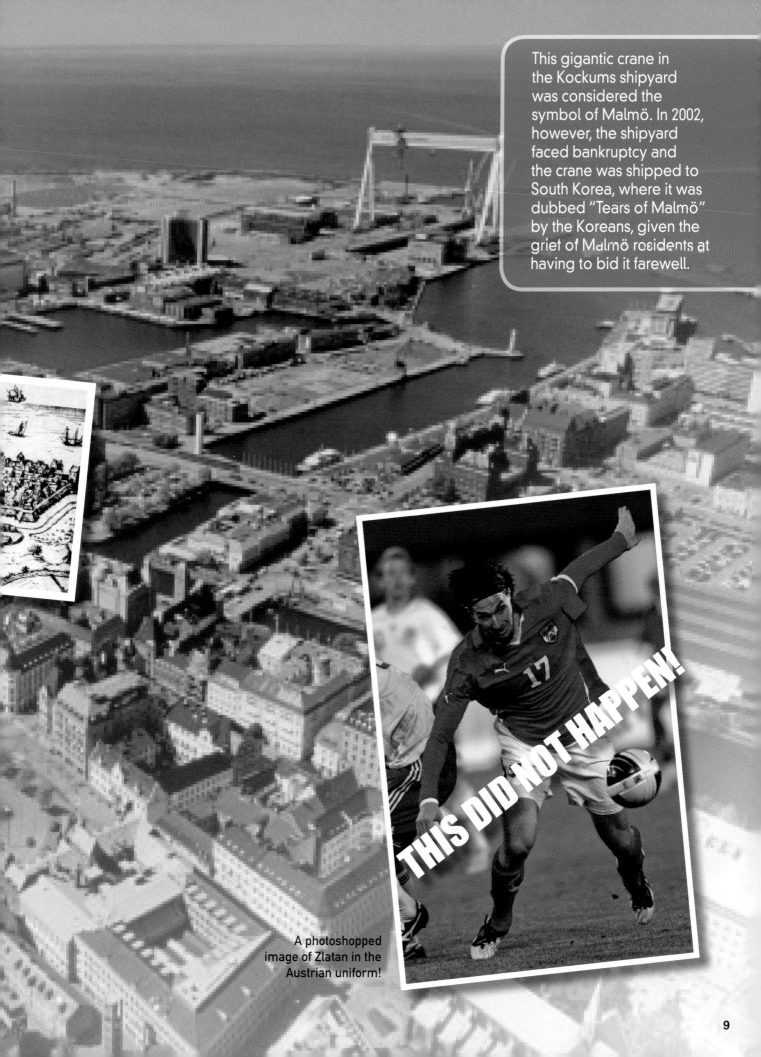

This gigantic crane in the Kockums shipyard was considered the symbol of Malmö. In 2002, however, the shipyard faced bankruptcy and the crane was shipped to South Korea, where it was dubbed "Tears of Malmö" by the Koreans, given the grief of Malmö residents at having to bid it farewell.

A photoshopped image of Zlatan in the Austrian uniform!

THIS DID NOT HAPPEN!

ROSENGÅRD

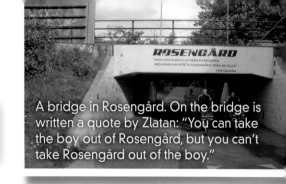

A bridge in Rosengård. On the bridge is written a quote by Zlatan: "You can take the boy out of Rosengård, but you can't take Rosengård out of the boy."

Around 1970, a new district was built in Malmö, called Rosengård. With time the district became populated mainly by immigrants and people of foreign origins. This was sometimes problematic. Many of the immigrants were poor. People did not always get along. And there is a great deal of unemployment in Rosengård. But there is also rich cultural diversity and often quite a lot of fun! Zlatan has always carried the torch of his old neighborhood, defended it in public and supported the residents in various ways. He is proud of being a boy from Rosengård.

In 2007 Zlatan funded the construction of a small soccer field in Rosengård—precisely where he began playing soccer as a child.

At the entrance it reads:

"Here is my heart. Here is my story. Here is my game. Keep it going. Zlatan."

Altogether 303,000 people live in Malmö. Of those 23,000 live in Rosengård.

A REBELLIOUS BUT FOCUSED KID!

Zlatan's father is named Sefik Ibrahimovic and is a Bosniak, a Muslim from Bosnia. He moved to Sweden in 1977 and his path crossed with a Croatian woman named Jurka Gravic. She is a Catholic like the majority of Croatians. They fell in love and later had Zlatan, a daughter Sanella, and a son Alexander. The family had to live from hand to mouth and occasionally the welfare authorities had to intervene. Zlatan's parents divorced, he acquired three more brothers, but everything went well in the end. Both parents were strict but gave their son a lot of freedom. And this Zlatan could appreciate.

When Zlatan was five years old he received his first soccer shoes, and when he began playing, he immediately showed great talent. He played for

Zlatan at the age of 8.

various youth squads in Malmö and once described how he entered a game when his teammates in FBK Balkan were losing 4–0 against Vellinge. But he turned the game around by scoring 8 goals!

Zlatan has often confessed that in his youth he could have found himself on the wrong path. He was boisterous and sometimes rebellious. But at heart he was organized and focused, and when he discovered soccer, the mastering of the sport became a conviction. In fact, he also practiced taekwondo as a teenager with excellent results and obtained a black belt. Zlatan's experience with taekwondo has without a doubt a lot to do with how quick and agile he is, despite his size.

Zlatan was not particularly industrious at school, though he clearly had a sharp mind. In the end, he dropped out of school in order to fully concentrate on soccer. It is said that at around the age of 15 Zlatan considered giving up soccer and starting work at the shipyard in Malmö.

This is hard to believe. A man of such talent, like Zlatan, would have always found his way straight back to soccer. And the biggest team in the city, Malmö FF, eventually got Zlatan on board.

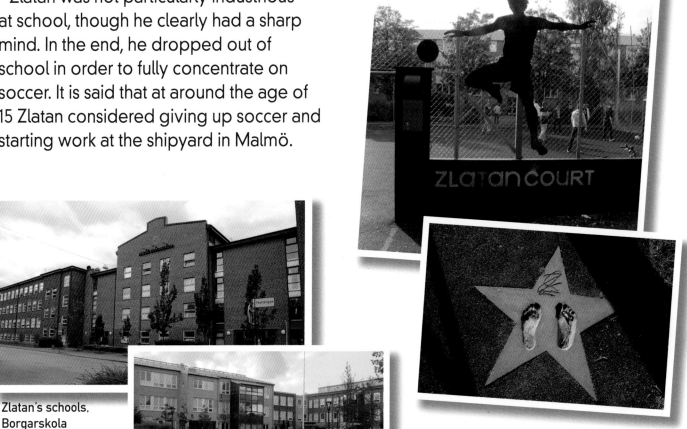

Zlatan's schools, Borgarskola (above) and the Stenkulaskolan elementary school.

Zlatan Court, the field which Zlatan funded. By the court is a print of his feet.

WHEN ZLATAN WAS BORN
October 3, 1981

In the year of 1981 Ronald Wilson Reagan was inaugurated as the 40th president of the United States.

Four days after Zlatan was born, the classic book *Ronia the Robber's Daughter*, by the cherished Swedish author Astrid Lindgren, was published. Later in October, a Soviet submarine was stranded by the shores of Karlskrona and gained international attention.

Prince Charles and Lady Diana got married in July. The original model of the IBM PC was released in August and was the most advanced, in the computer industry.

Anwar Sadat, the president of Egypt, was murdered, but an attempt on Ronald Reagan's life failed.

The first 24-hour video music channel MTV was launched.

LIBRA

Zlatan belongs to the star sign Libra according to astrology. Libra spans from September 22 to October 23 each year. Scientists claim that there is no sense in astrology though many people still enjoy it. Those who are Libras are considered first and foremost calm and even-tempered. They are also outgoing and go out of their way to make others feel comfortable. In addition, they are good-natured and can't stand bullying or rudeness. How does this fit Zlatan?

It is rather interesting that the man who is supposed to score the goals for the Swedish national team, and the man defending against the opponent's goals, were both born on the same day.

On the same day that Zlatan entered the world in Malmö, another boy was born in Smygehamn, which is close to the city Trelleborg. He has been the main goalkeeper for the Swedish national team for the last decade. His name is Andreas Isaksson. He began his career in Sweden with Trelleborg FF and then played with Djurgården IF until joining Rennes in France in 2004. From the years 2006 to 2008 Isaksson was a goalkeeper for Manchester City, and in his second season there was under the command of Swedish coach Sven-Göran Eriksson.

After his time in Manchester, Isaksson transferred to Holland to play with PSV Eindhoven.

Andreas Isaksson

From there he moved to Turkey in 2012 where he plays with Kasimpasa.

Andreas has taken part in over 100 international matches for Sweden and he and his birthday brother, Zlatan, have celebrated many victories together.

13

THE GOLDEN ONE

The name Zlatan came from the Balkans, where this master of soccer originated. The name is particularly popular in Bosnia and Herzegovina because three different ethnic groups live in that country: Bosniaks, Croatians, and Serbs. And the name Zlatan is "neutral"— in other words, all three groups use the name equally. The name therefore does not indicate which group a particular boy belongs to.

The name simply means "golden" and is drawn from the word "zlato," which means gold.

IBRAHIMOVIC means "son of Ibrahim." The suffix "ic" or "vic" in the name comes from Eastern Europe, and means son. And the name Ibrahim was originally an Arabic translation of the Biblical name Abraham. A Nordic version of the name Ibrahimovic would therefore be something along the lines of Abrahamson.

THE OTHER TWO ZLATANS

The fact that two other talented Swedish-Bosnian players bear the name Zlatan shows just how popular the name is among people of Bosnian descent.

ZLATAN MUSLIMOVIC was born in 1981 in Bosnia. He arrived in Sweden with his family in 1993 as a refugee from the civil war which raged there. As a young man, he played for IFK Gothenburg and other teams, but later moved to Italy where he played for years. After playing in Greece for three years Muslimovic joined the team Guizhou Renhe in China. Muslimovic plays with the Bosnia and Herzegovina national team and had at the end of August 2013 played 30 international matches and scored 12 goals.

ZLATAN AZINOVIC was born in 1988 in Kalmar, and is of Bosnian descent. He is a goalkeeper who has played Kalmar FF, Trelleborg FF, and Malmö FF. Azinovic played with youth squads in Sweden with great success.

WHERE DOES HE

Zlatan's father comes from Bosnia and Herzegovina but his mother is from Croatia. Both are small countries in the Balkans. Along with other neighboring countries they were a part of one nation, which until 1990 was called Yugoslavia. Many nationalities and ethnicities lived in Yugoslavia. Even though the nations were related and spoke similar languages the country began to break apart in 1991. Unfortunately, this caused many conflicts and wars between the newly formed nations and within them. Croatia was at war with Serbia who tried to prevent Croatia from becoming an independent nation. One of the worst situations was in Bosnia and Herzegovina where Bosniaks, Serbs, and Croatians fought cruelly for years. The civil war finally ended in 1995.

The war did not harm Zlatan directly, but of course it was very difficult for everyone of Bosnian descent to observe the atrocities of war in their home country.

In the end, seven new countries were formed from the remains of Yugoslavia: Slovenia, Croatia, Serbia, Bosnia and Herzegovina, Montenegro, Macedonia, and Kosovo.

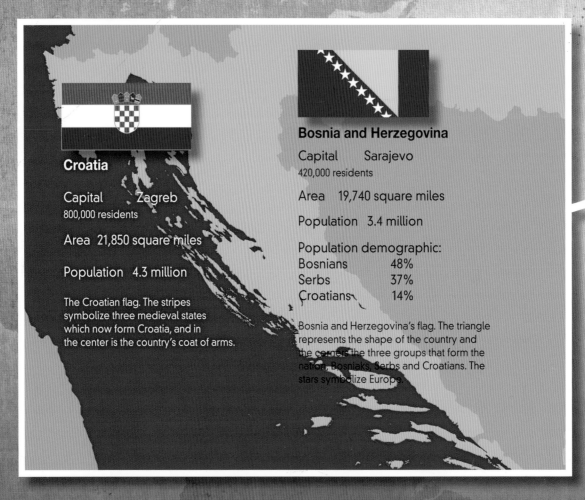

Croatia

Capital   Zagreb
800,000 residents

Area   21,850 square miles

Population   4.3 million

The Croatian flag. The stripes symbolize three medieval states which now form Croatia, and in the center is the country's coat of arms.

Bosnia and Herzegovina

Capital   Sarajevo
420,000 residents

Area   19,740 square miles

Population   3.4 million

Population demographic:
Bosnians   48%
Serbs   37%
Croatians   14%

Bosnia and Herzegovina's flag. The triangle represents the shape of the country and the corners the three groups that form the nation, Bosniaks, Serbs and Croatians. The stars symbolize Europe.

COME FROM?

STRONG SOCCER NATIONS

Soccer became very popular in Yugoslavia very early on. The national team participated in major tournaments with good results. In 1992, Yugoslavia had secured their place in the European Championship League held in Sweden. At the last minute, however, they were forbidden from taking part because of the war in their country. Denmark was then summoned in their place, 10 days before the tournament began. And very surprisingly, Denmark became the European champions after defeating Germany in a final match at the Ullevi Stadium in Gothenburg.

After Yugoslavia was dismantled, the new countries had shown great promise, especially Croatia, who finished third at the 1998 World Cup. Bosnia and Herzegovina have not yet reached the finals of a big tournament, but is getting increasingly stronger by the day. These days, the best player for Bosnia and Herzegovina is Edin Dzeko, striker for Manchester City.

Edin Dzeko is a very talented goal scorer.

MALMÖ FF

Malmö FF was founded in 1910. During the 1943–1944 season, Malmö FF won its first championship in the top Swedish league, Allsvenskan, and has won the championship 19 times, more often than any other team in the league.

In the 1978–1979 season Malmö FF achieved the biggest success of all Swedish teams in the European Cup, which is now called the UEFA Champions League. After victories over the French team Monaco, the Soviet team Dynamo Kiev, and the Polish team Wisla Kraków,

Malmö Stadium, Malmö FF's home ground 1958–2009.

Malmö FF reached the semifinals where they played Austria Wien. The first match in Austria ended scoreless, but at Malmö Stadium Tommy Hansson scored the goal which secured Malmö FF a place in the final. The final was held at the Olympiastadion in Munich, and there Malmö narrowly lost 1–0 against the English team Nottingham Forest.

The last decade of the 20th century saw a brief decline for Malmö FF. In the summer of 1999 the unthinkable happened, the team was demoted from the 1st division to the 2nd division.

Around the same time, a young and promising soccer player was smashing his way through the youth ranks: Zlatan Ibrahimovic.

Roland Andersson took over as coach of Malmö FF in 1998. At the time Zlatan played with the team's youth squad. Once, Andersson went to see the youth team practice and finally signaled Zlatan to come and speak with him. Zlatan describes what happened next in his autobiography. Andersson told him that he had to stop playing soccer with the kids.

Zlatan's heart sank. He thought that he had made some mistake and was now being kicked out of the team. Instead, what Andersson meant of course, was that Zlatan was becoming so good that should join the main team.

In his book, Zlatan writes that he has rarely in his life been so proud. And since Zlatan was such a mischievous young man at that time, he celebrated by stealing a bike and having a blast with it.

He felt he was the coolest person in Malmö!

Zlatan played in 6 matches with the main team in the season of 1999. The team was then still in the Allsvenskan. He scored one goal, against Vastra Frölunda, on October 30, shortly after turning 18 years old. The following summer he played with Malmö in the second highest soccer league

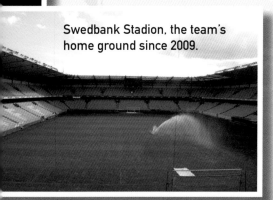

Swedbank Stadion, the team's home ground since 2009.

in Sweden and racked up 12 goals in 26 matches. His talents were now obvious.

When the season of 2001 began, Malmö FF was back in the Allsvenskan. Zlatan kept scoring and after 8 games he had scored 3 goals. By now it was becoming obvious that he had, in fact, outgrown Malmö FF. The big European teams had their eyes on this striking Swede. In July, Zlatan was off to Amsterdam in Holland, having been bought by the renowned Ajax team.

Zlatan during the Malmö FF game against Helsingborg in the Swedish Cup in November 2000.

IN THE YELLOW JERSEY!

Because of his parents' origins, Zlatan could have played for either Bosnia or Croatia. But for him that was never really an option. He would only play for the country of his birth. When he was nearing twenty, he had already gained the attention of national team coaches Lars Lagerbäck and Tommy Söderberg, who led the national team together at the time. Zlatan played in his first international game on January 31, 2001, when he had just reached the age of nineteen. The match was a part of the last Nordic Soccer Championship, and the opponents were from the Faroe Islands. The game ended scoreless. The next day, Zlatan played against the Finns. This is apparently the only time Zlatan has played two real soccer matches two days in a row.

On the October 7, 2001, Zlatan played his first real competitive match. Sweden was playing Azerbaijan in the qualifying tournament for the 2002 World Cup. Zlatan came on as a substitute in the 66th minute. It did not take long for him to make his mark on the game because he managed to score the third and last goal for Sweden after only three minutes on the field.

Zlatan soon became indispensable for Sweden. The main hero of the team was Henrik Larsson, who became good friends with Zlatan, despite a ten-year age difference.

The success of the Swedish national team has tended to fluctuate. Sometimes fine victories have been won but then the team seems to stumble at the last hurdle.

Zlatan scored a magnificent goal against Italy in the 2004 European Soccer Championship. It was chosen the best goal of the tournament. He also scored a brilliant goal against France in Euro 2012.

Erik Hamrén, coach of the national team since 2009, made Zlatan the captain of his team. This showed just how important the big striker had become for the team. At the end of August 2013, Zlatan had played 91 international matches, scoring a total of 44 goals.

The goal against Italy in UEFA Euro 2004:
During a chaotic confrontation in the penalty area, Zlatan miraculously managed to chip the ball with his back heel into the net. Zlatan's taekwondo training may have come in handy here.

The goal against France in UEFA Euro 2012:
Sebastian Larsson gave a long pass from the right flank and Zlatan flew into the air, caught the ball in mid-air and smashed it directly into France's net. An utterly fabulous goal, yet another proof of Zlatan's skill.

On October 17, 2012, Zlatan scored the first goal in a remarkable comeback, when the Swedish team drew 4–4 with Germany after having been down 4–0.

Henrik Larsson and Marcus Allbäck celebrate with Zlatan after his majestic goal at the UEFA Euro 2004.

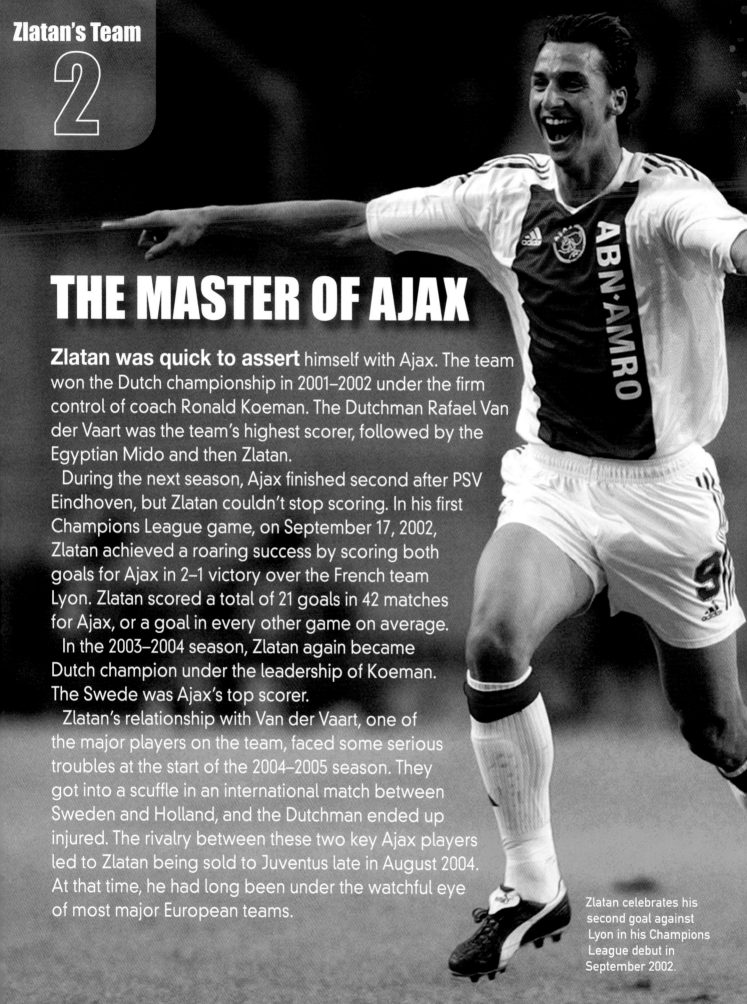

THE MASTER OF AJAX

Zlatan was quick to assert himself with Ajax. The team won the Dutch championship in 2001–2002 under the firm control of coach Ronald Koeman. The Dutchman Rafael Van der Vaart was the team's highest scorer, followed by the Egyptian Mido and then Zlatan.

During the next season, Ajax finished second after PSV Eindhoven, but Zlatan couldn't stop scoring. In his first Champions League game, on September 17, 2002, Zlatan achieved a roaring success by scoring both goals for Ajax in 2–1 victory over the French team Lyon. Zlatan scored a total of 21 goals in 42 matches for Ajax, or a goal in every other game on average.

In the 2003–2004 season, Zlatan again became Dutch champion under the leadership of Koeman. The Swede was Ajax's top scorer.

Zlatan's relationship with Van der Vaart, one of the major players on the team, faced some serious troubles at the start of the 2004–2005 season. They got into a scuffle in an international match between Sweden and Holland, and the Dutchman ended up injured. The rivalry between these two key Ajax players led to Zlatan being sold to Juventus late in August 2004. At that time, he had long been under the watchful eye of most major European teams.

Zlatan celebrates his second goal against Lyon in his Champions League debut in September 2002.

WORLD FAMOUS!

One could claim that Zlatan first reached the heights of world fame when he scored a brilliant goal against NAC Breda on August 22, 2004. He got the ball just outside Breda's penalty area, and weaved his way through a barricade of five defenders, before finally sliding the ball elegantly past the goalkeeper. Eurosport's viewers selected the goal as the greatest one of the year. This goal clearly showed the most remarkable thing about Zlatan: Even though he is tall and heavily built, he can display a level of skill and dexterity that legends like Pelé or Maradona would happily settle for.

Zlatan wearing the uniform of Juventus in a friendly match against Barcelona in August 2005.

WITH THE OLD LADY

Juventus goes under the name of the "Old Lady" and the fans of the old-timer were ecstatic when Zlatan joined her ranks. He scored a goal in his first league match wearing the "bianconeri" jersey and the team's coach, Fabio Capello, was certainly very impressed. Zlatan played a lot and in the spring of 2005 it turned out he was Juve's highest scorer of the season, with a total of 16 league goals. Next in line was veteran Alessandro del Piero with 14, and then the Frenchman David Trezeguet with 9.

Diligently helped by Zlatan, Juventus became Italian champions with AC Milan coming in second.

In the following season, Capello moved Zlatan more to the wings. Trezeguet was the main striker and racked up the goals with the aid of Zlatan and others. Still, Zlatan scored ten goals himself.

Again Juventus became the champions of Serie A with AC Milan the runner-up. Zlatan and his teammates were described as playing glorious soccer. However, as the season concluded, a major scandal emerged. A number of soccer clubs, including Juventus and AC Milan, had participated in a scheme with corrupt referees to fix the results of certain matches. Fortunately, the players themselves were not involved in the scandal. But Juventus was stripped of the two titles won over the previous seasons and pushed down to Serie B, the second highest league in Italy.

Many of the Old Lady's key players understandably did not want to play in the Serie B and therefore left for other teams. Among these players was Zlatan. The Old Lady tried emphatically to keep him, to no avail.

HOW TALL IS HE?

Height under the bar: 8 feet

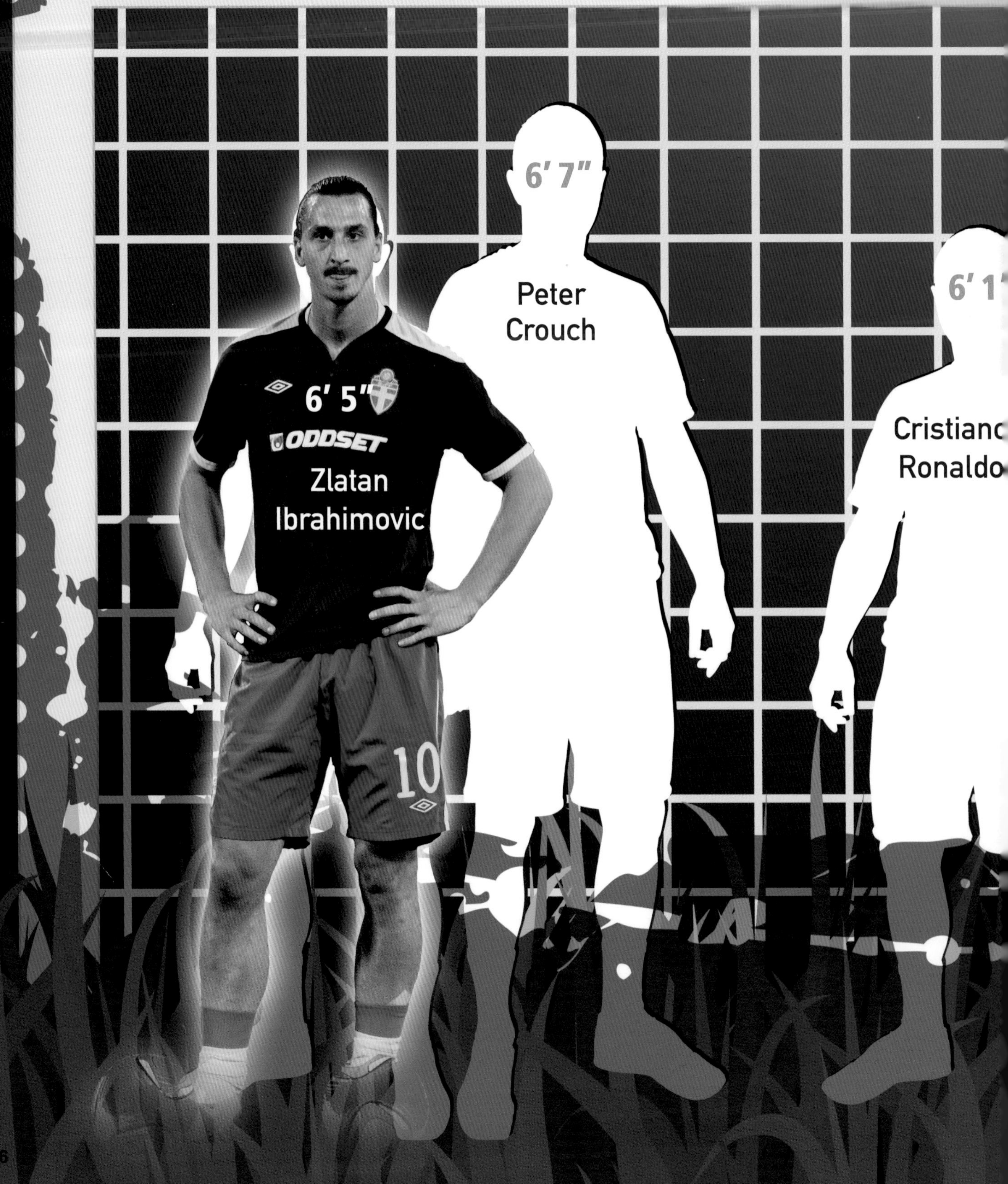

6' 7"

Peter
Crouch

6' 5"

Zlatan
Ibrahimovic

6' 1"

Cristiano
Ronaldo

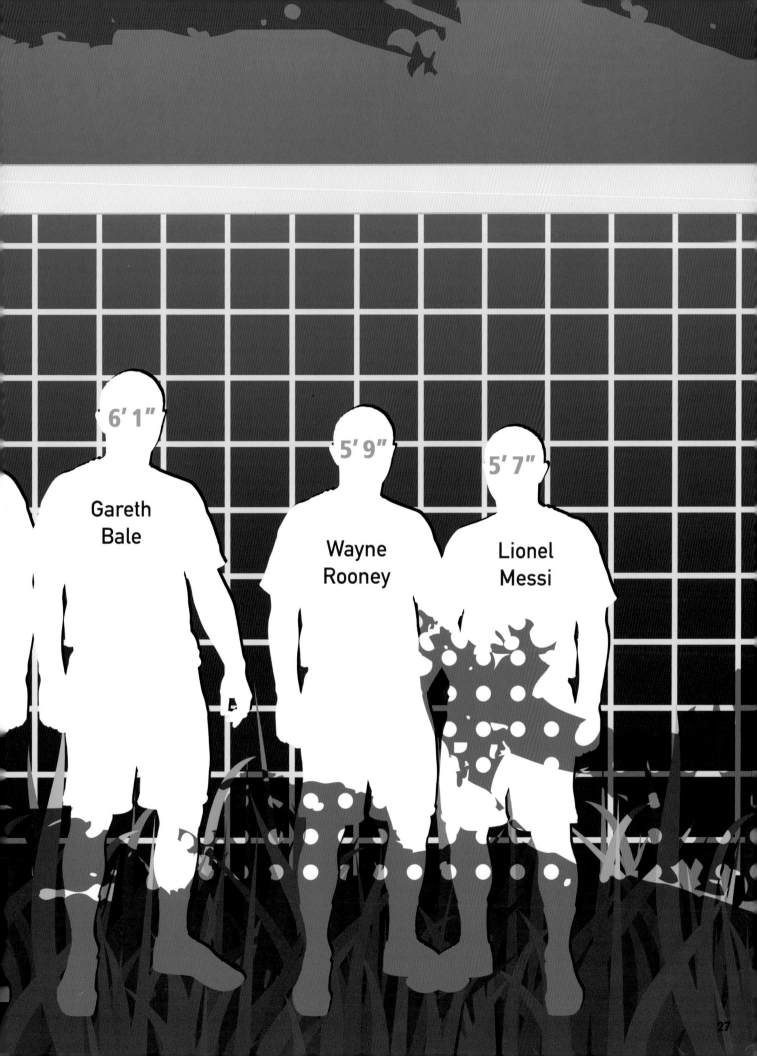

6' 1"

Gareth
Bale

5' 9"

Wayne
Rooney

5' 7"

Lionel
Messi

RECORD GOALS

Zlatan's old dream came true when he joined Inter Milan. That was what he had dreamt about back home in Rosengård. And he certainly played boldly. In the 2006–2007 season Inter became the Italian champions for the first time in 17 years, led by coach Roberto Mancini, and Zlatan was the top scorer on the team with 15 goals. Inter's superiority was great and the team won 17 matches in a row at one point.

The next season, 2007–2008, Inter won the Italian championship again, and again Zlatan was the top scorer.

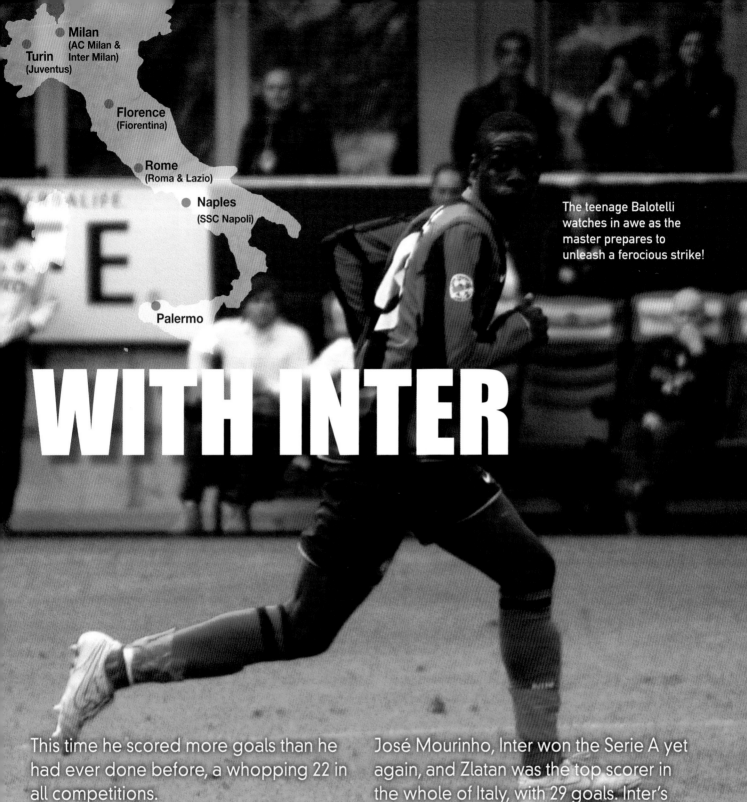

Milan
(AC Milan & Inter Milan)

Turin
(Juventus)

Florence
(Fiorentina)

Rome
(Roma & Lazio)

Naples
(SSC Napoli)

Palermo

The teenage Balotelli watches in awe as the master prepares to unleash a ferocious strike!

WITH INTER

This time he scored more goals than he had ever done before, a whopping 22 in all competitions.

If someone had by now been in doubt as to whether Zlatan had already entered the ranks of the world's best soccer players, this skepticism dissolved into thin air during his third season with Inter, 2008–2009. He simply couldn't stop scoring goals! Under the leadership of a new coach, the famous and controversial

José Mourinho, Inter won the Serie A yet again, and Zlatan was the top scorer in the whole of Italy, with 29 goals. Inter's second highest player scored only 10 goals.

That was young and promising Mario Balotelli.

When the season was over, Zlatan was sold for a record amount to the greatest soccer club of recent years, Barcelona in Spain. Still more successes beckoned.

ZLATAN'S MANSION

When Zlatan was a penniless youth in Rosengård, he claims to have dreamily wandered around the affluent neighborhoods of Malmö on a bike that he didn't own. A pink colored mansion by Limhamnsvägen always caught his attention. He thought the house was magnificent and always wondered what kind of people lived there.

In 2007 Zlatan had become rich and world famous and he and his wife, Helena Seger, began to look around for a house in Malmö. In Zlatan's autobiography he writes: "We made a list of all the best houses and what house do you think landed on top of the list? The pink villa on Limhamnsvägen! And not just because of my old dreams. The house was truly the greatest. It was the most beautiful house in Malmö but there was one problem. People lived in the house and they didn't want to move. What do you then do?"

In the end, Zlatan managed to make the residents of the house an "offer they couldn't refuse," as he says himself with reference to the film *The Godfather.* Helena and Zlatan got the house for 4 million dollars. It is claimed that another 4 million went into restorations.

Whether or not Zlatan and Helena will settle for good in the Limhamsvägen villa, this respectable house still remains an intriguing chapter in the tale of the Rosengård boy who conquered the world.

THE MANY FACES OF ZLATAN

Zlatan is very strict in relation to alcohol and doesn't touch drugs of any kind.

Even though Zlatan always seems very confident nowadays, in his younger days he was often very nervous before important games.

A teammate of his with Malmö FF said that sometimes Zlatan threw up in the locker room from sheer nervousness. But with time he learned how to tame his anxiety and found a way to vent it on the field.

The Swedish national team players were once asked who the most important athlete in Swedish history was. Many famous names were mentioned, such as the NHL star Peter Forsberg, the tennis player Björn Borg among others. Zlatan was the only one who named a woman, Annika Sörenstam, the

greatest female golfer in recent times.

Though Zlatan is now in his thirties he still preserves the boy inside. In his home there is a special room in which there is a top-quality TV and stereo system of the most expensive kind. Zlatan sits in front of the screen and plays video games with no less concentration and dedication than he plays soccer.

It might be surprising to someone that the hard-shelled Zlatan has a quite sophisticated and even "soft" taste in music.

Among his favorite musicians are:

Halid Beslic, a Bosnian singer who makes music in true Bosnian spirit. Songs like *Miljacka* and *Cardak* touches a chord with anyone who traces their roots to Bosnia or neighboring countries.

Alpha Blondy from the Ivory Coast who plays reggae music infused with African folk music and other genres. Check out his song, *Jerusalem*, on YouTube.

And then there is the Serbian pop singer Ceca with the song *Ja jos spavam u tvojoj majici*, which means "I am still sleeping in your shirt."

Which means of course: "I have still not got over you" or something like that.

However, Zlatan has also been known to occasionally blast hard rock through his stereo, like the heavy metal band AC/DC and some others in the same category.

SONGS ABOUT ZLATAN

Zlatan does not just enjoy listening to music, he has himself become the subject of song. Three songs have been written about Zlatan.

In the summer of 2006 the band Elias was a big hit with the song, *Who's da Man*, which the youthful Frans Jeppsson-Wall sang.

In the same year the Malmö rapper Demis Tzivis made a bit of a tougher song where he raps: "Thanks man, you give us all hope / all of us from Rosengård."

In 2008, the band the Ballerinas & the Pendletones came out with the song *Zlatan and I*. The singer rejoices about being from Malmö just like his idol, Zlatan.

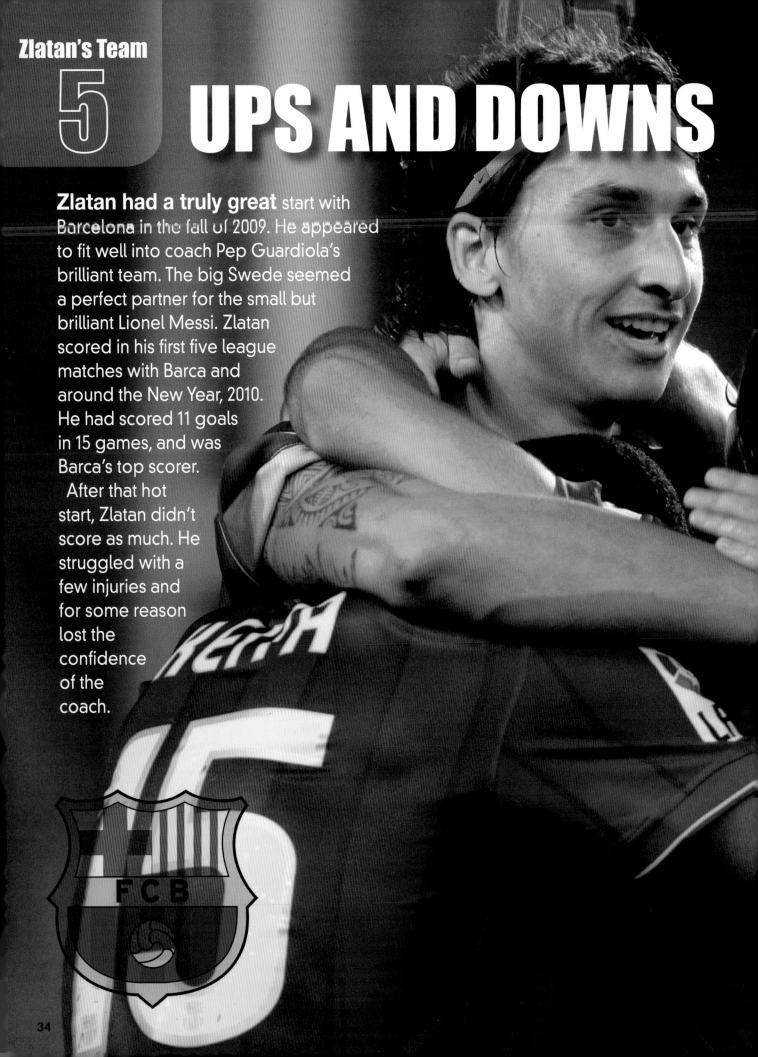

5 UPS AND DOWNS

Zlatan had a truly great start with Barcelona in the fall of 2009. He appeared to fit well into coach Pep Guardiola's brilliant team. The big Swede seemed a perfect partner for the small but brilliant Lionel Messi. Zlatan scored in his first five league matches with Barca and around the New Year, 2010. He had scored 11 goals in 15 games, and was Barca's top scorer. After that hot start, Zlatan didn't score as much. He struggled with a few injuries and for some reason lost the confidence of the coach.

WITH BARCELONA

Zlatan became very disappointed with Guardiola during this difficult period. He didn't speak to his troubled striker for months and offered no help. Even so, Zlatan wound up the season with 21 goals, which is of course a very good performance. And he became a Spanish champion and won a number of other titles with the team.

The biggest disappointment was perhaps when Barca lost in the semifinals of the Champions League against Zlatan's old team Inter.

When the summer of 2010 arrived it was clear that the trust between Zlatan and Guardiola had been lost. At the beginning of the following season the Swede packed his bags and moved to Italy again, this time to Inter Milan's bitter rival, AC Milan.

Iniesta   Messi   Xavi

"I COULDN'T BE MYSELF"

Zlatan has always spoken highly about the talents of his Barcelona teammate Lionel Messi. However, in his autobiography, *I am Zlatan*, he writes that he thought Messi and some of his teammates were too submissive to the inhospitable coach Guardiola: "Messi, Xavi and Iniesta did as they were told without questioning. They are like a bunch of schoolboys. I am not like that. I couldn't be myself."

THE CARS

PORSCHE CARRERA GT

Zlatan has always been heavily interested in cars and the salary he receives for playing soccer provides him with the means to afford more cars, and more expensive cars, than most others. Here are some of the luxury cars he has owned over the years.

FERRARI 360 SPIDER

VOLVO C30 T5

PORSCHE CAYENNE TURBO

FERRARI ENZO

NEVER BETTER

Though his time at Barcelona was much shorter than originally planned, Zlatan kept his stride and continued his victorious goal scoring march with AC Milan during the 2010–2011 season. Led by the coach Massimiliano Allegri, the team won the Serie A league championship in Italy, and Zlatan became a champion for the eighth year in a row, and with his fifth club.

Along with the Brazilians Pato and Robinho, Zlatan formed Milan's dangerous front line and the Swede became the top scorer. Zlatan scored the only goal in a great victory for Milan over his old team, Inter Milan, who were AC Milan's main competitors for the Serie A championship.

In the following season, 2011–2012, Zlatan did even better and scored more than he had ever done before, 35 goals in 44 matches! Sadly, this was only enough to secure Milan second place in Serie A. Zlatan, however, proved that he was like good wine, still improving with age!

And meanwhile in Paris, the Swedish master was being carefully observed and when the summer of 2012 arrived, a French team made their move. Soon, Zlatan, was on his way to Paris St. Germain.

Zlatan was not the first
Swede to make his mark
with AC Milan. In the 1950s,
three Swedes won great fame
with the club, and played a
significant role in making
AC Milan one of Europe's
strongest teams. Above, left
to right: Gunnar Gren (with
Milan 1949–1953, 38 goals),
Gunnar Nordahl (1949–1956,
221 goals), and Nils Liedholm
(1949–1961, 89 goals). In his
most successful season, 1949–
1950, Nordhal scored 35 goals,
exactly the same amount as
Zlatan, over 60 years later.

TATTOOS

Like many other athletes, Zlatan likes tattoos. One could even say that he played a role in popularizing tattoos among athletes. When this book was written, Zlatan has a total of 20 tattoos. And they all carry a meaning.

Zlatan has the name of his father, Sefki, tattooed on his right arm along with the names of his sons. Their birthdays as well as those of all of Zlatan's brothers are scribbled on the front side of his upper arm.

His mother's name, Jurka, is written on the inner side of his left arm (close to the heart) and her date of birth, along with his sister's, Sanela, are tattooed on the upper left arm. Zlatan dubs the birthday tattoos as "The Ibrahimovic Code."

On the back side of his upper arm the Ibrahimovic family name is written in Arabic, in honor of his father's roots.

On the front side of his right upper arm there is tattoo of a symbol from the Maori in New Zealand, which is supposed to protect Zlatan and his family.

Then there is an ace of spades (a symbol for the search for knowledge) and ace of hearts on the right side of Zlatan's torso. Inside the ace of hearts one can glean an "H" which doubtlessly refers to the love of his life, Helena Seger.

The Japanese koi fish on his left shoulder symbolizes Zlatan's masculinity. The fish is concentrated and brave, and swims against the stream.

The polygonal star drawn on his lower back is derived from Eastern Buddhism and represents the elements. This symbol defends Zlatan against disease.

The symbol resting on the upper side of his back is called *Yant Prajao Khao Nirote* and also comes from Buddhism and protects against suffering.

The eagle's feather on the middle of his back is probably a symbol for bravery.

The red dragon on the right side of his torso stands for Zlatan's fighting spirit.

Also, on the right side of his body there is written: "Only God Can Judge Me."

Lastly, Zlatan has a tattoo of his name on the lower side of his belly but it is rather obscure and can rarely be seen.

THE FAMILY

Zlatan's wife is Helena Seger. She comes from a small town close to the city of Örebro. In the beginning of her career, Helena was a popular model and actress in Sweden but has since then been engaged in a variety of marketing and business projects. She is eleven years older than Zlatan but the age difference has never been an issue in their relationship. They share a similar sense of humor and their interests are also alike.

Helena and their two sons watch Zlatan play in a match with AC Milan against Genoa on April 25, 2012. The boys are named Maximilian (to the left), born in September 2006, and Vincent, born in March 2008.

THE MOST EXPENSIVE ONE

When AC Milan sold Zlatan to Paris Saint-Germain, it was clear that he had become the most expensive soccer player in history at the start of the 2012–2013 season. It is rather difficult to calculate the exact amount of money that changes hands when soccer clubs purchase players, but the information on this page is at least close to being accurate!

1. Zlatan Ibrahimovic

Malmö – Ajax	9.7 million dollars
Ajax – Juventus	20 million dollars
Juventus – Inter Milan	32 million dollars
Inter Milan – Barcelona	97 million dollars*
Barcelona – AC Milan	30 million dollars
AC Milan – Paris St. Ger.	29 million dollars

A total of almost 220 million dollars!

* The contract between Inter and Barca was quite complicated but it is estimated at this amount.

2. Nicolas Anelka, France

Arsenal – Real Madrid – Paris St. Germain – Liverpool – Manchester City – Fenerbahce – Bolton – Chelsea – Shanghai Shenua

173 million dollars

3. Hernán Crespo, Argentina

River Plate – Parma – Lazio – Inter Milan – Chelsea – Inter Milan – Genoa – Parma

156 million dollars

4. Juan Sebastian Veron, Argentina

Estudiantes – Boca Juniors – Sampdoria – Lazio – Manchester United – Chelsea – Inter Milan – Estudiantes

151 million dollars

5. Cristiano Ronaldo, Portugal

Sporting – Manchester United – Real Madrid

143 million dollars

6. Ronaldo, Brazil

Cruzeiro – PSV Eindhoven – Barcelona – Inter Milan – Real Madrid – AC Milan

130 million dollars

7. Bale, Wales

Southampton – Tottenham – Real Madrid

128 million dollars

8. Robbie Keane, Ireland

Wolves – Coventry – Inter Milan – Leeds – Tottenham – Liverpool – Tottenham – Los Angeles

121 million dollars

9. Christian Vieri, Italy

Atalanda – Juventus – Atlético Madrid – Lazio – Inter Milan

113 million dollars

10. Samuel Eto'o, Cameroon

Real Madrid – Mallorca – Barcelona – Inter Milan – Anzhi Makhachkala (Russia) – Chelsea

At least 110 million dollars

Zlatan receives 17 million dollars per year with PSG. In addition, he receives money from advertising and from other sources.

Zlatan is therefore one of the highest paid soccer players in the world.

When Christiano Ronaldo claimed to be "unhappy" at Real Madrid in late 2012, it was thought that his unhappiness was due to Zlatan's extraordinary salary at PSG. The Swede had become an economic threat to him, as well as a soccer rival!

A number of politicians in France publicly declared that it was unethical that one person could receive such a high salary for playing soccer.

Others, however, were happy that Zlatan would move to France and pay his high taxes there.

ZLATAN

A FANTASTIC GOAL!

On the November 14, 2012, the new Swedish national stadium in Stockholm, Friends Arena, was inaugurated with a friendly match between Sweden and England. Zlatan was simply astounding and scored all 4 goals in Sweden's 4–2 victory. The final goal is considered one of the most beautiful goals in history, an overhead kick from almost 40 yards. Watch it on YouTube over and over again!

S RAIN OF GOALS!

HERE WE ACCOUNT FOR ALL THE GOALS ZLATAN HAS SCORED IN PUBLIC GAMES WITH HIS SOCCER CLUBS BEFORE THE 2013–2014 SEASON.

269 Goals!

In addition to the 6 goals in 7 U21 internationals, and 44 goals in 91 internationals, a total of 51 international goals!

		Matches	Goals
MALMÖ FF	1999	6	1
	2000	26	12
	2001	8	3
Total		**40**	**16**
AJAX	2001-02	33	9
	2002-03	42	21
	2003-04	31	15
	2004-05	4	3
Total		**110**	**48**
JUVENTUS	2004-05	45	16
	2005-06	47	10
Total		**92**	**26**
INTER MILAN	2006-07	36	15
	2007-08	34	22
	2008-09	47	29
Total		**117**	**66**
BARCELONA	2009-10*	45	21
Total		**46***	**22***
AC MILAN	2010-11	41	21
	2011-12	44	35
Total		**85**	**56**
PSG	2012-13	46	35
TOTAL		**536**	**269**

• Zlatan played one game with Barca in the beginning of the 2010–2011 season and scored one goal. This is accounted for here.

7

THEY DEMANDED ZLATAN

Nasser Al-Khelaifi and Leonardo introduce Zlatan.

In 2011, an investment company from Qatar in the Persian Gulf bought the storied French club Paris Saint-Germain. The former professional tennis player Nasser Al-Khelaifi became the president of the club. He began his reign by funneling huge amounts of money into the club and hired the best personnel available. The Brazilian Leonardo became the director of soccer and the Italian Carlo Ancelotti was hired as head coach. They began to gather the best players they could find and they didn't cease until AC Milan agreed to sell them the mighty Zlatan!

ANCELOTTI

was born in 1959. He played as a midfielder for Parma and Roma but his greatest success was achieved with AC Milan. Twice he became a European champion with the team. He then took to coaching and AC Milan won the UEFA Champions League twice under his leadership from 2001 to 2009. He then moved to Chelsea for a time. During the summer of 2013 Ancelotti left PSG for Real Madrid. He was replaced by French World Cup veteran Laurent Blanc.

Carlo Ancelotti is one of the world's most clever coaches.

LEONARDO

was born in 1969. He was a regular player for the Brazilian national team in the last decade of the 20th century. Leonardo played a total of 60 international matches and scored 8 goals. He began as a left back but later moved into midfield. For a time, Leonardo played for PSG but also for AC Milan. After he retired from playing soccer, he was for a time the coach of both AC Milan and Inter Milan, but then transferred to PSG. In August 2013 he left PSG.

In his first 6 games with PSG, Zlatan scored 8 goals! Altogether he scored 35 goals in 46 games during the first season. PSG became French champions!

A YOUNG MEGA-TEAM

Paris Saint-Germain is one of the youngest superclubs of Europe. It wasn't founded until 1970 when two smaller clubs in Paris joined forces. The team entered the highest league in France, Ligue 1, in 1974, and has since then been among the strongest teams.

They first won the league title in 1985–1986 and then again in 1993–1994. This was first won in 1985–1986 and then again 1993–1994. After that, the title eluded PSB time and again. The team won the French Cup eight times, however, and thrice the French League Cup. And in 1996 PSG won the UEFA Cup Winners' Cup.

The ambitious plans of the new owners paid off. PSG became champion by a comfortable margin in 2012–13, not least due to the spectacular performance of Zlatan who again and again led his team to victory.

FAMOUS PSG PLAYERS

		PSG Year	Matches	Goals
Carlos Bianchi	Argentina	1977–78	80	71
George Weah	Liberia	1992–95	137	55
Youri Djorkaeff	France	1995–96	47	20
Nicolas Anelka	France	1995–97 2000–02	69	19
Ronaldinho	Brazil	2001–03	77	25
Pauleta	Portugal	2003–08	211	110

Weah won both the Golden Ball as the best soccer player in Europe and FIFA's award for the world's best player while he was with PSG. Ronaldinho was the most expensive player that PSG has ever sold. Barcelona paid 32 million euros for him in 2003. Pauleta is PSG's all-time leading scorer.

THE EIFFEL TOWER AND THE CRADLE OF THE KING

On PSG's crest is an image of the Eiffel Tower, the symbol of Paris, and under the tower there is a stylized image of the cradle of King Louis XIV (1643–1715). The cradle is the symbol for the Saint-Germain district of Paris, because this is where the "Sun King" was born.

PARC DES PRINCES

The home of PSG is called Parc des Princes, which means "the park of princes." During the 18th century, the park was used for relaxation only by royal princes. A soccer field was inaugurated in the park in 1897. The present stadium was completed in 1972. It is renowned for the noise produced by roaring fans of PSG in support of their favorite team. The opponents of PSG fear the ruckus, not least when the fans chant in unison: "Ici c'est Paris," or "This is Paris!"

The stadium has seating capacity of almost 49,000 spectators. PSG has been offered an even bigger venue in Paris, Stade de France (81,000 people) but refuses to leave its traditional home.

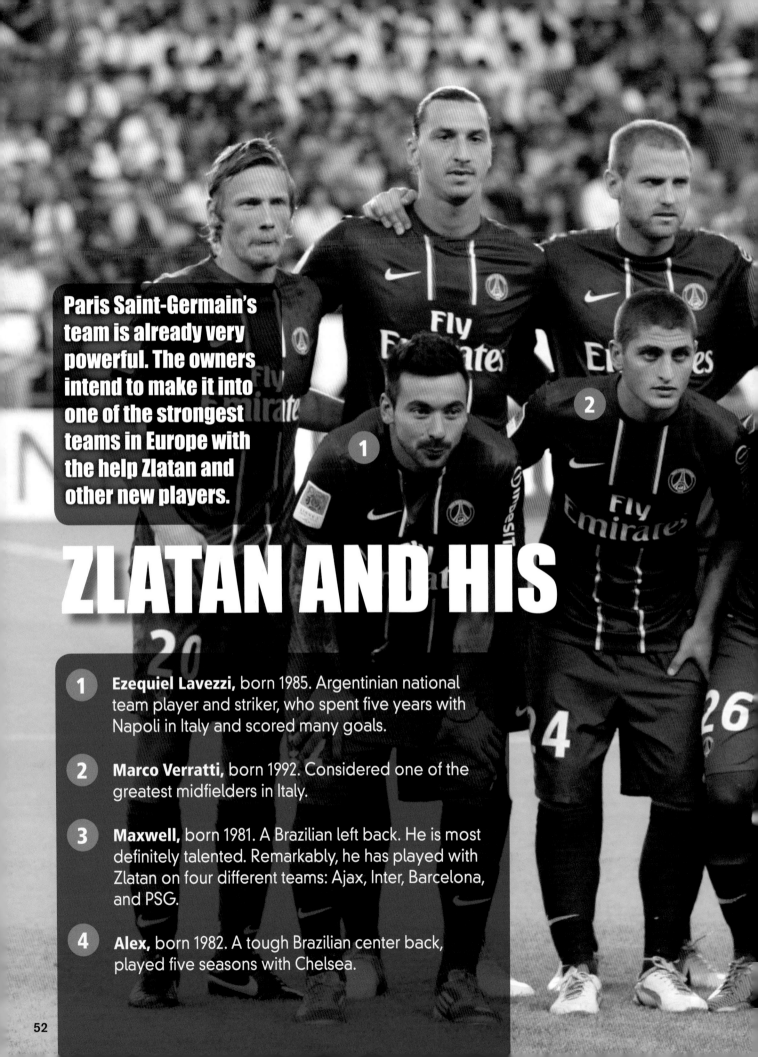

Paris Saint-Germain's team is already very powerful. The owners intend to make it into one of the strongest teams in Europe with the help Zlatan and other new players.

ZLATAN AND HIS

1 **Ezequiel Lavezzi,** born 1985. Argentinian national team player and striker, who spent five years with Napoli in Italy and scored many goals.

2 **Marco Verratti,** born 1992. Considered one of the greatest midfielders in Italy.

3 **Maxwell,** born 1981. A Brazilian left back. He is most definitely talented. Remarkably, he has played with Zlatan on four different teams: Ajax, Inter, Barcelona, and PSG.

4 **Alex,** born 1982. A tough Brazilian center back, played five seasons with Chelsea.

TEAMMATES IN PARIS

OTHER GREAT PLAYERS

Thiago Silva, born 1984. A center back from Brazil, arrived to PSG from AC Milan in 2012 along with Zlatan. Cost 42 million euros. Began his career with the Brazilian national team rather late but is now a key player there and considered one of the world's greatest players. Refused a move to Barcelona in 2013.

Javier Pastore, born 1989. A bold attacking midfielder from Argentina and considered to have vast potential. Scores and racks up the goals. Moved from Palermo in Italy for 40 million euros in 2011.

Lucas Moura, born 1992. A Brazilian attacking midfielder. Came from Sao Paulo in 2012–2013. He is thought to be one of the most promising soccer players in the world: light, agile, and full of skill.

AS TOUGH AS NAILS

Zlatan is not always easy to get along with, neither for the opponents nor his teammates.

"He kind of mocks you. The first time I faced Pauleta, I conceded three goals. In the first game against Lisandro, I conceded three goals as well. Ibrahimovic scored two goals in 21 minutes ... He's just as good as they are ... When he moved towards me, alone, I felt like I had closed the goal. But he always finds a way to get the ball in the back of the net."

Mickael Landreu, Lille goalkeeper after facing Zlatan and PSG on September 2, 2012.

"If I have to be honest, playing with Zlatan was never easy. You had to approach him carefully. The secret is to pass him the ball, or he starts to shout at you, or play tricks on you afterwards."

Stephan El Shaarawy, young Italian striker who played and trained with Zlatan at AC Milan.

The Future

The adventure of Zlatan

Ibrahimovic has become an epic one. Originating from the southern Balkans but born in the northern country of Sweden, growing up in Rosengård, definitely not with a silver spoon in his mouth, he learned to be tough and to stand on his own feet. Departed for the south, first to Holland where he showed the world that a new master had entered the scene, and then to Italy, where the game of soccer is of the highest quality in the world. There, Zlatan entered the ranks of the most skillful and most prominent strikers in the world, and his impeccable skill became obvious to all.

When he arrived in Barcelona he was recognized as one of the world's greatest soccer players. Zlatan's reaction to the hardships he was confronted with in the second part of his season with Barcelona clearly showed that not only was he a man of talent, but also a man of character, who doesn't allow anything to break him. With AC Milan he managed to have some of his greatest seasons, and at the age when some soccer players give up their game, Zlatan set sail for new adventures on the banks of the Seine. Adventures which will possibly award him one of the few prizes he hasn't already won, the Champions League. There is no shortage of ambition with Paris Saint-Germain or with Zlatan. But whether his stay with the Parisian team is his last soccer adventure or not is something no one can tell, except Zlatan himself. He says he's determined to win all possible awards and trophies with PSG, and teaming up with new PSG striker Edinson Cavani from Uruguay might just bring the ultimate reward!

Zlatan is a hot-tempered man, focused and honest. He travels his own paths and doesn't allow anybody to prevent him from doing so. He is not an easy opponent. But at the same time he is loyal to his close friends and stays in good contact with his parents.

At the beginning of Zlatan's career he had a tendency to be a bit unreliable and erratic, prone to drift out of games and sometimes he failed to assert himself. But Zlatan overcame these shortcomings. Now no one can doubt that the towering Swede gives it all he's got.

Of course! He is Zlatan after all!

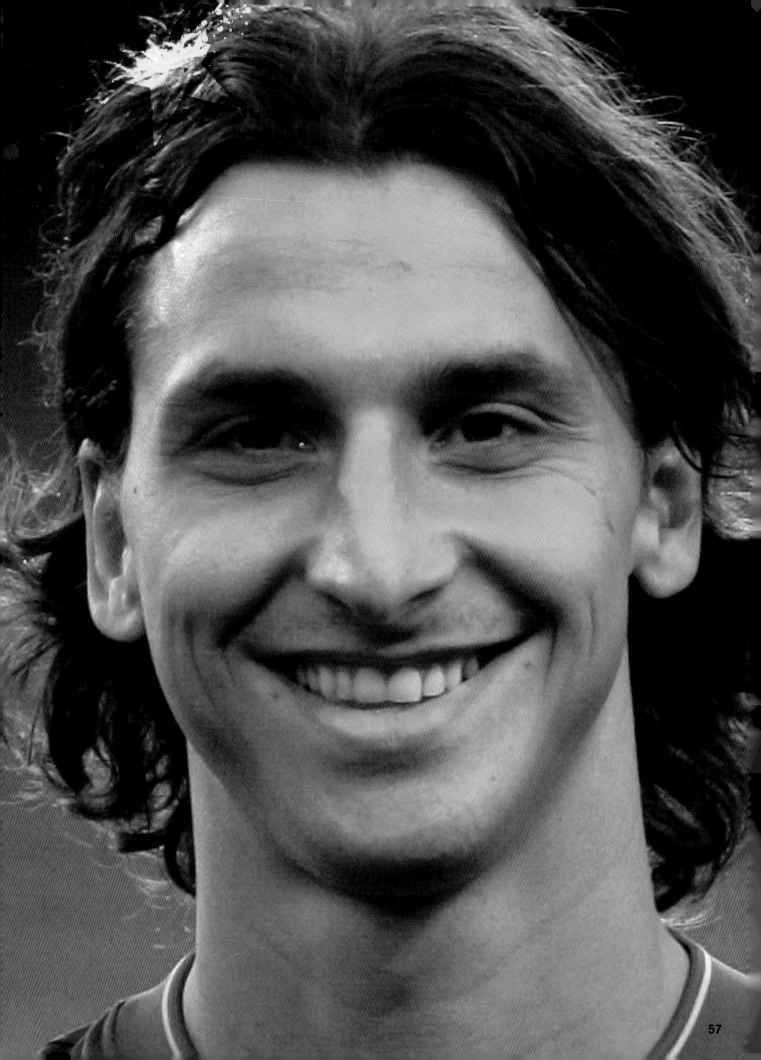

Zlatan still has many matches to play if he wants to outdo other Swedish international team players. Thomas Ravelli played 143 matches from 1981 to 1997. Anders Svensson had played a total of 142 international games from 1999 until August 2013. At that time Zlatan had played "only" 91! However, Zlatan has joined the ranks of Swedish top scorers. Sven Rydell scored 49 goals from 1921–1932 but Zlatan has already scored 44 and probably wants to score a few more! In third place is Gunnar Nordahl with his 43 goals from 1942–1948 and Henrik Larsson scored 37 goals from 1993–2009.

LIVING LEGEND

On September 10, 2012, Zlatan got his own slab on Malmö's "Walk of Fame" outside the Malmö stadium. It was no question that this event delighted the dynamic master.

"It is often said that you cannot become a legend until you die. But now I am a living legend—at least in Malmö," Zlatan exclaimed with a gleaming smile on his face at a press conference after the slab had been unveiled.

"This means a lot to me. After 10 years of struggling, having given them (the fans) so much, and getting so much in return. I would happily give much more than I accept myself. This memorial is deeply touching. It is in a way proof that you have achieved something in your life. I will always remember this. I can tell my children about this ... it's a wonderful feeling, but it is hard to describe."

So even the big talker himself is sometimes speechless!

Learn More!

Books
- *I am Zlatan Ibrahimovic*, by Zlatan Ibrahimovic, David Lagercrantz, and Ruth Urbom
  A boisterous and fun autobiography.

Websites
- The Wikipedia entry on Zlatan holds an abundance of information about the the player, his life, and teams.

- His own website is very useful too: ibrahimoviczlatan.com/.
- espnfc.com (Soccernet)
- goal.com
- 101greatgoals.com
- fourfourtwo.com
- zlatanfan.com (A fan site)

Glossary

Striker: A forward player positioned closest to the opposing goal who has the primary role of receiving the ball from teammates and delivering it to the goal.

Winger: The player who keeps to the margins of the field and receives the ball from midfielders or defenders and then sends it forward to the awaiting strikers.

Offensive midfielder: This player is positioned behind the team's forwards and seeks to move the ball through the opposing defense. They either pass to the strikers or attempt a goal themselves. This position is sometimes called "number 10" in reference to the Brazilian genius Pelé, who more or less created this role and wore shirt number 10.

Defensive midfielder: Usually plays in front of the team's defense. The player's central role is to break down the offense of the opposing team and deliver the ball to their team's forwards. The contribution of these players is not always obvious but they nevertheless play an important part in the game.

Central midfielder: The role of the central midfielder is divided between offense and defense. The player mainly seeks to secure the center of the field for their team. Box-to-box midfielders are versatile players who possess such strength and foresight that they constantly spring between the penalty areas.

Fullback (either left back or right back): Player who defends the sides of the field, near his own goal, but also dashes up the field overlapping with wingers in order to lob the ball into the opponent's goal. The fullbacks are sometimes called wing backs if they are expected to play a bigger role in the offense.

Center back: These players are the primary defenders of their teams, and are two or three in number depending on formation. The purpose of the center back is first and foremost to prevent the opponents from scoring and then send the ball towards the center.

Sweeper: The original purpose of the sweeper was to stay behind the defending teammates and "sweep up" the ball if they happened to lose it, but also to take the ball forward. The position of the sweeper has now been replaced by defensive midfielders.

Goalkeeper: Prevents the opponent's goals and is the only player who is allowed to use their hands!

Pick Your Team!

Coach:

_____

Who do you want to play with Zlatan? Choose a team for him. Don't forget the coach!

Goalkeeper:

_____

Right back:

_____

Left back:

_____

Defender:

_____

Defender:

_____

Midfielder:

_____

Midfielder:

_____

Midfielder:

_____

Forward:

_____

Forward:

_____

Striker:

Zlatan

The Zlatan Board Game!

You start from Rosengård

2

You score 8 goals with the youth squad. Jump 8 squares ahead!

You join Malmö FF. Another turn!

5

You fail to score in the first national game. Wait 1 round

You are bought by Juventus. Go to square 11

Play with one die.

8

You are sent off for protesting. Go back 4 squares

To win, players decide whether you have to land exactly on the final square or not.

You pro spon bac

1

You move to Inter Milan and you are an immediate hit. Do taekwondo kick and throw the dice again

You are sold to Barcelona for 60 million euros. Count to 60 and throw again

12

You score goals in the first 5 matches. Move squares ahead